City Zoo Adventures with Dyamond and Vesta

Frizella Taylor

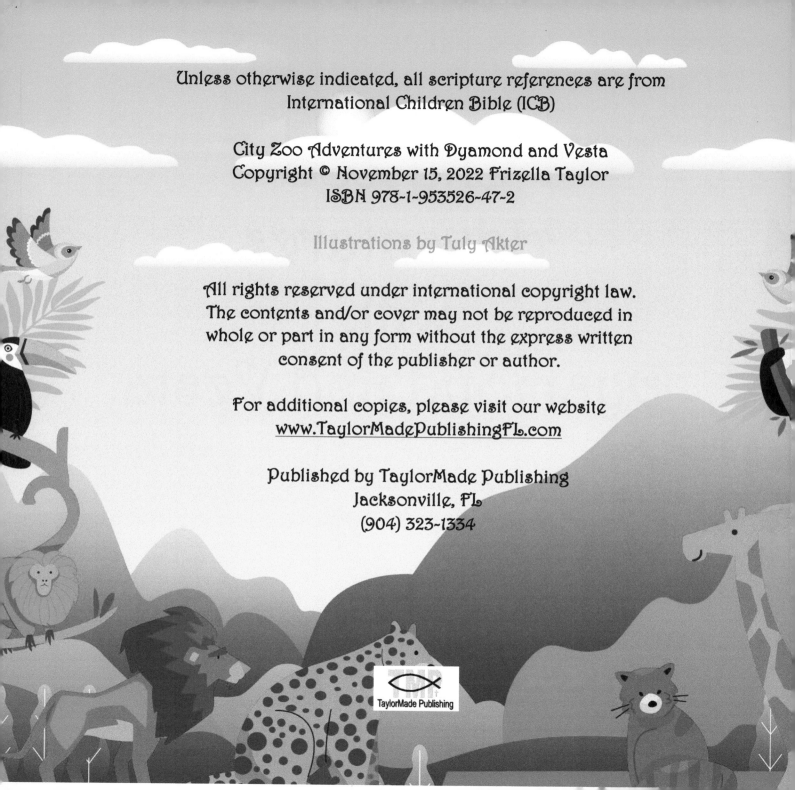

Unless otherwise indicated, all scripture references are from
International Children Bible (ICB)

City Zoo Adventures with Dyamond and Vesta
Copyright © November 15, 2022 Frizella Taylor
ISBN 978-1-953526-47-2

Illustrations by Tuly Akter

For additional copies, please visit our website
www.TaylorMadePublishingFL.com

Published by TaylorMade Publishing
Jacksonville, FL
(904) 323-1334

TMP
TaylorMade Publishing

Table of Contents

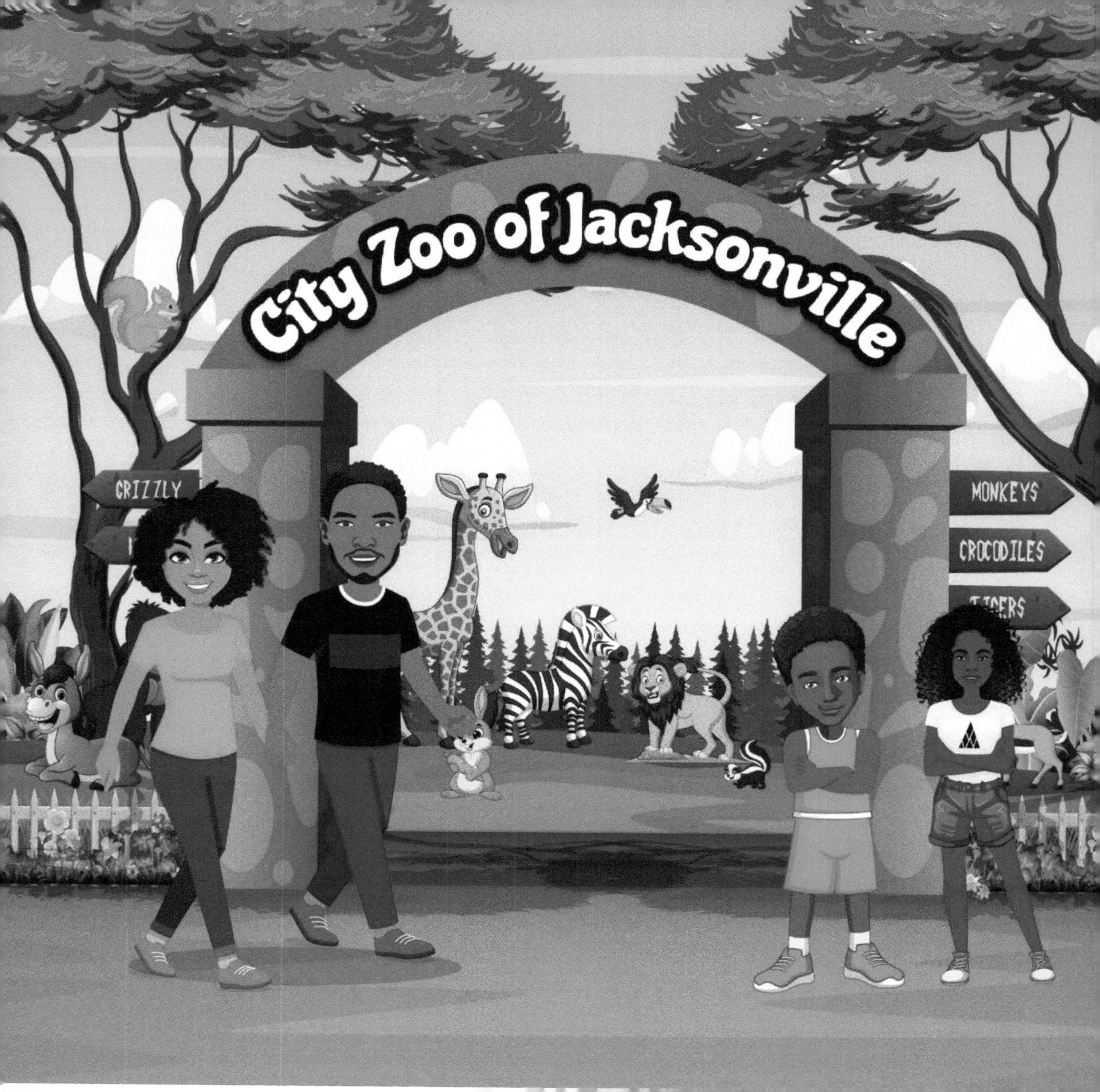
City Zoo of Jacksonville
GRIZZLY
MONKEYS
CROCODILES

1: Introduction

Dyamond and Vesta's entire classroom had the same summer assignment. They each had to visit the city zoo and report on all the animals they could identify.

Dyamond and Vesta were excited because they had not been to the zoo in quite a while. So, mommy and daddy were prepared to take them early on a bright Saturday morning.

But before they could head out, they had to get prepared for the trip. They all had tasks they had to complete before they could go to the City Zoo.

2: Let's Get Ready!

It was 7:00 o'clock on Saturday morning.
Mommy was up preparing lunch baskets
for the big day at the city zoo.

The sun was bright and shining through
the kitchen windows.

Mommy had bottles of water, cartons of
juice, and several kinds of sandwiches.
She had apples, oranges, and cookies for
everyone to snack on.

Mommy was happy to prepare the
food for her family trip to the zoo.

[3]

In the meantime, daddy was busy cleaning
out the minivan and washing it.
Daddy was listening to his favorite praise song,
"This is the day, this is the day,
the Lord has made; I will rejoice, I will rejoice,
and be glad in it."

His neighbor Mr. David, spoke to him from across the
street, "Good morning Mr. Joseph, God bless you!"

Mr. Joseph spoke back, "Good morning Mr. David,
blessings to you and have a fantastic day! "

Mr. David asked, "Are you heading out today?"

Mr. Joseph replied," Yes we are taking the children
to the city zoo today!"

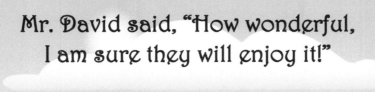

Mr. David said, "How wonderful,
I am sure they will enjoy it!"

Mr. Joseph replied, "I hope so, seeing that it is
a school project, nevertheless, we will do our
best to make it a fun adventure for them."

Mr. David said, "Oh wow! That will be
great, enjoy your day!"

Mr. Joseph replied, "Thank you! You do the same."

Mr. Joseph continued cleaning out his minivan.

Dyamond finished her bathroom duties and
straightened up her bedroom.

She got dressed in her favorite jean shorts,
T-shirt, and comfy sneakers.

She took one last look in the mirror
to check out her outfit before leaving her room.

Dyamond said to herself,
OK, you're looking good. "I am ready." she said, and
proceeded out of her bedroom to find her mom.

[9]

Vesta was rushing to get done in his
room because he woke up a little late.

Vesta shouted to Dyamond,
"Wait for me I am almost done."

He grabbed his gym shoes in his hand,
as he ran out of his bedroom.

He got to the staircase and realized
he did not have socks, so he quickly
ran back into his room for socks.

Vesta grabbed a pair of socks
and headed back to the staircase
to catch up with Dyamond.

[11]

3: Come On, Let's Go!

Finally, everyone in the house was ready
and daddy called for them to load up
in the minivan.

Mommy carried the lunch baskets and
loaded them into the back of the van.

Daddy took the cooler of water
and juice out and loaded them in the van.

Dyamond and Vesta grabbed their rain coats;
because in Florida it is common to have splash
and dash rain showers throughout the day.

The family all loaded into the minivan
and before they started off daddy said
let's pray. Daddy began to pray...

"Heavenly Father, I thank you for this beautiful day.
I pray for sunshine, beautiful weather, and
a great experience for my children.

Father, I ask for safe travel to the
City Zoo and that there will be no accidents.

Please allow Dyamond and Vesta to have
fun as well as learn about the many
animals you created.

In Jesus' name. Amen."

[15]

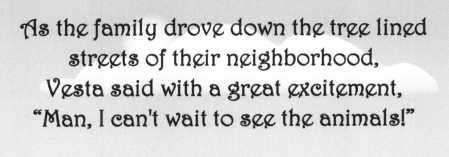

As the family drove down the tree lined
streets of their neighborhood,
Vesta said with a great excitement,
"Man, I can't wait to see the animals!"

Dyamond sighed at him and said,
"Vesta just be patient, we will get there,
you are just too excited."

Vesta said, "Well aren't you excited too?"
You got up really early to get here ready."

Dyamond said, "I was up early to make sure
my hair and my clothes looked good."
Vesta said, "Yeah right!" and started laughing...

[17]

city zoo entrance

Daddy was approaching the tall bridge that was just before the exit to the City Zoo entrance.

Both Dyamond and Vesta got excited and leaned towards their windows to see the water and the ships.

Vesta said, "Wow, this is so awesome! The ships are really big!"

Dyamond replied, "Yes, they are! I can see the beautiful sun shining across the blue waters".

Mommy joined in and said "Yes, it is refreshing to see some of God's creations."

[19]

Mommy said, "Did you all know God created all the animals? And saved them from the great flood?"

Diamond said, "My Sunday school teacher was telling us about it a few weeks ago."

Vesta said, "Really? I have not heard that story before. I want to know more about the animals they seem to be really cool."

Mommy said, "Yes in Genesis chapter 7, God told Noah that he was a good man and he and his family were to go into the Ark. Noah was also told by God to take seven pairs of every kind of animal both clean and unclean onto the Ark. He was also told to take seven pairs of all the birds in the sky onto the Ark." All of the pairs were to be male and female in order for the animals to remain on the earth after the flood.

[21]

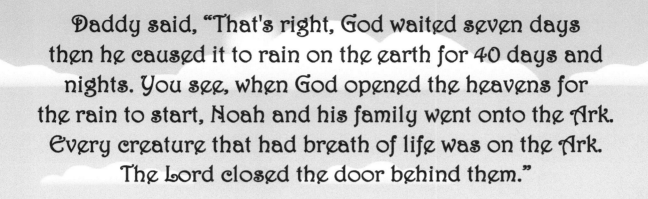

Daddy said, "That's right, God waited seven days then he caused it to rain on the earth for 40 days and nights. You see, when God opened the heavens for the rain to start, Noah and his family went onto the Ark. Every creature that had breath of life was on the Ark. The Lord closed the door behind them."

Vesta said, "Wow that was cool and scary at the same time. I am glad I was not there when that happened. I don't think I would have liked it very much"

Mommy said, "God caused it to rain long enough for the Ark to float. Then the rain stopped, and the water started going down."

[23]

Daddy said, "Noah needed to be sure there was dry land to walk on. So, he sent a Raven out and then a Dove, but no dry land was found, and the Dove returned. When Noah sent the Dove again after seven days it returned with an olive leaf indicating dry land. Once on dry land, God told Noah and his family to leave the boat along with all the animals and birds and everything that crawls on the earth. God told Noah they should
have many young ones and grow in numbers."

Mommy said, "So you see, when you visit the animals in the city zoo today you will understand how they got to live so long among us.

Dyamond and Vesta were so happy their parents shared that Bible story with them.

[25]

City Zoo of Jacksonville

GRIZZLY

HYENAS

MONKEYS

CROCODILES

TIGERS

4: Arriving at the City Zoo

Dyamond and Vesta were so excited when they saw the City Zoo signs as they were exiting the bridge. The sign pointed towards the zoo entrance.

Daddy said, "OK kids we are about to arrive at the City Zoo, do you have your notebooks and pencils so that you can take notes about the animals you see?"

They both answered, "Yes Daddy we have our notebooks and pencils, and we also have our cell phones."

Mommy said, "I want you kids to be on your best behavior. Remember, while this is a fun trip it is also a homework assignment. You can use your cell phones to take pictures of the animals you see.

[27]

Dyamond said, "Do I have to stay with Vesta? Because we need different animals for our school report.

Mommy said, "That is a good point, so Dyamond why don't you and I go to the right, to look at the animals."

Daddy said, "Vesta you and I will go to the left and find the animals in that direction."

Dyamond said, "Great mommy, I would love to see if we can find the African Lion, they have great hair like me."

Vesta said, "Cool daddy, can we find the giraffes because I'm gonna be tall like them when I grow up."

Daddy said, "OK we have a plan, so let's meet up in 2 hours in the picnic area for lunch."

[29]

City Zoo of Jacksonville

GRIZZLY

HYENAS

MONKEY

CROCODIL

TIGERS

So, Dyamond and mommy headed toward the right side of the zoo. While Vesta and daddy went toward the left side of the zoo.

Dyamond said, "Mommy I think I am going to really enjoy our time together. I will get to learn about many animals with you."

Mommy said, "Yes I agree, I love mommy and daughter time we get an opportunity to bond."

Dyamond said, "Look mommy, it's the lion sign, let's go that way!"

Mommy said, "okay, slow down, don't bump into people."

[31]

They got to the lion exhibit and saw
several lions roaming around and roaring.
Some of the younger kids were afraid and covered
their ears, clung to their parents and some even cried.

The lion's roar was so loud that even the
birds scattered from the trees. But Dyamond was
fascinated by it. She pulled out her cell phone
and took some pictures and wrote notes
in her notebook about the lions.

Dyamond and mommy went from one exhibition
to the next taking many pictures and writing lots
of notes in her notebook.

Dyamond was so happy to be with her
mommy for this special school project.

Meanwhile, Vesta and daddy were on the other side of the city zoo was. Daddy was telling Vesta a story about when he went to the zoo with his parents when suddenly...

Vesta said, "Hey daddy, can we go see the giraffes first? They are my most favorite animal."

Daddy said, "Absolutely, but if we see other animals along the way we can include them in your report too."

Vesta said, "OK that is a good idea."

So, Vesta and daddy headed toward the left side of the City Zoo. Just as they were turning into the next gate...

Vesta said with excitement, "Daddy look! There are some gorillas can we go see them!"

[35]

Daddy said, "Yes we can go over to see them. Don't get too far ahead of me."

Vesta said, "Wow! They are huge! I wonder how much that gorilla weighs?"

Daddy said "Vesta take out your notebook, you see the sign here, write down the information. It has some details you can add to your report."

Vesta, said, "Yes, I see! It's just what I need, and I am going to take some pictures of this gorilla he is amazing."

Daddy and Vesta continued on to each exhibit along the way taking pictures and writing notes in his notebook.

Vesta was really enjoying his visit to the City Zoo with his dad.

After the family had been walking around
seeing the animals and taking pictures,
they bumped into each other.

Mommy said, "Hey look, there is daddy and Vesta!

Dyamond shouted, "Daddy, Vesta over here!"

Vesta shouted back, "Hey Dyamond, we are coming!"

Daddy said, "Hey, let's get lunch and compare notes."

Daddy and Vesta went to the minivan to get the
basket of sandwiches and the cooler of drinks.

Mommy and Dyamond went to the
picnic area to find a table.

5. What Did You Learn?

The family sat down at the picnic table,
each of them grabbed a sandwich, fruit, and
a cold water and a juice box.

Mommy said, "Wow kids! That was an adventure.
I am sure you all have great pictures
and notes, right?"

Daddy said, "And you had fun as well, right?"

Vesta said, "Oh yes that was the best homework
assignment I ever had!"

Dyamond said, "I actually agree with Vesta, the
best homework assignment, and yes, it was
adventurous as well as so much fun!"

Mommy said, "That is good to hear!
I really enjoyed it myself too! It was so much fun."

Daddy said, "Yes it was great! But other than the animals, I
want to know what you kids liked the best before
you start talking about the many animals you saw."

Vesta said, "Other than the animals, I enjoyed just
being out in the open air and the warm sun."

Dyamond said, "I feel the best part of this adventure
was mommy and I hanging out together. I just love it
when we can be alone together and she was a big help
identifying the animals with me."

Mommy said, "Oh Dyamond it was my pleasure,
you know we can hang out together anytime you like."

Vesta said, "OK you two are being mushy again!
Daddy and I always have a great time, we just
don't have to say it like you guys say it."

Daddy said, "Alright, alright, everyone let's
hear what you learned about some of
the animals from the exhibits today.
Who wants to go first?"

Mommy said, "Yes let's do that while
I put away the uneaten food.
I am curious to hear all about your
experiences with the animals!"

[45]

6. Vesta's Animal Presentations

Vesta said, I can go first...these are the animals I found at the City Zoo for my report. The giraffe is my favorite"

Reticulated Giraffe
Size:
Males weigh between 1700-4000 lbs. and females from 1200-2500 lbs. Giraffes are the tallest of all animals and can grow to 18 feet tall.
Diet:
Giraffe likes to eat leaves and shoots of trees and shrubs
Habitat:
Northeastern Kenya, eastern Sudan and Eritrea in open woodland and wooded grassland areas.

Western Gorilla
Size:
Male up to 500 Lbs. Females up to 216 Lbs.
They can reach up to 6 feet on two legs.
Diet:
Gorillas eat a vegetarian diet, of stems
bamboo shoots and fruits.
Habitat:
Western gorillas live in lowland, swamp, and
montane forests from sea level to 1600 m
(5249 ft)

Guereza Colobus Monkey
Size:
Head and body length – 18 to 27 in; tail length –
20 to 35 in; weight – 15 to 30 lbs. At birth,
newborns are approximately 8 inches long and
weigh less than 1 lb.
Diet:
Leaves and Fruits
Habitat:
Inhabit equatorial areas of Africa and S Sudan.
In woodlands, wooded grasslands and montane
forests

Bonobo Pan paniscus
Size:
Male up to 86 Lbs. Females up to 68 Lbs. The male grows up to 2.72 ft and female grow to 2.49ft
Diet:
Bonobos eat fruits but also leaves seeds, grass, and small animals.
Habitat:
Lowland rainforests of central Congo (Kinshasa)rainforest.

Rhinoceros Hornbill
Size:
The rhinoceros' hornbill is a large arboreal hornbill, 31–35 in long. The weight varies by sex, with males weighing 87.0–104.4 oz and females 72–82 oz.
Diet:
Fruits, small mammals, lizards, snakes, and insects
Habitat:
Malay peninsula, western Indonesia, Borneo Java, and Sumatra

[49]

Komodo Dragon
Size:
Grows up to 10 feet and can weigh 150-300 lbs
Diet:
Invertebrates, birds, and mammals
Habitat:
Indonesian islands, including Komodo, Rintja, and western Flores living in tropical island forests and beaches

Bald Eagle
Size:
Female body is 35 – 37 in wing span 35-37 in. Male body is 30-34 in and wing span 72-85 in. Weight varies from 10 to 14 lbs.
Diet:
Primarily fish but also birds and small mammals
Habitat:
Throughout North America near forest, lakes, rivers and coastal marshes

Eastern Bongo
Size:
Height: 3.9 to 4.2 feet at the shoulder;
weight: males – 529 to 890 lbs., females –
462 to 560 lbs.
Diet:
Leaves, shoots, flowers, twigs of shrubs,
vines, and thistles
Habitat
Central and West Kenya in forest
through the bamboo and moorland

American Black Bear
Size:
Adult males typically weigh between
126–551 lb, while females weigh 33%
less at 90–375 lb
Habitat:
North America local forest in Ocala
National Forest ad Big Cypress
Swamp among swamps, bogs,
Everglades, and riverine forests.

Aldabra Giant Tortoise
Size:
One of the largest land tortoises, second only to the Galapagos tortoise. Males can weigh up to 550 pounds, while females can weigh up to 350 pounds.
Diet:
Invertebrates, birds, and mammals
Habitat:
Indonesian islands, including Komodo,

American Alligator
Size:
On average length of between 6 and 10 feet, with males rarely reaching 12 - 14 feet. The tail length is almost half of their overall length.
Diet:
Fish, turtles, birds, snakes, frogs, and mammals
Habitat:
Southeastern United States near freshwater lakes, ponds and rivers

7: Dyamond's Animal Presentations

Dyamond said, "These are the animals I found at the City Zoo for my report. The lion is my favorite."

African Lion

Size:
Adult male lion stands almost 4 feet at the shoulder and is 5.6 to 6.3 feet long. Average weights vary from 330 to 550 lbs. Tail length averages 3.3 feet long. Females are considerably smaller and weigh less than 300 lbs.
Diet:
Large and medium sized mammals, birds and small mammals
Habitat:
Sub-Sharan Africa in Savanna, scrublands, and open woodlands.

Cheetah
Size:
Height: 27 – 35 in.; weight: 77 – 143 lbs.
The fastest land animal running up to 80 mph
Diet:
Carnivore that hunts small to medium-sized prey weighing 44 to 132 lb, but mostly less than 88 lb. Its primary prey are medium-sized ungulates.
Habitat:
Near East to southern India and across Africa and central Iran in most habitats

African Elephant
Size:
Height: 27 – 35 in.; weight: 77 – 143 lbs.
Diet:
a range of plants, including grasses, fruit, roots, leaves, and branches
Habitat:
Sub-Saharan Africa, where they inhabit Sahelian scrubland and arid regions, tropical rainforests, mopane and miombo woodlands. tropical island forests and beaches

[55]

Grevy's Zebra
Size:
8.2–9.0 ft in head-body with a 22–30 in tail and stands 4.8–5.2 ft high at the withers. They weigh 770–990 lb.
Diet:
Grasses and leaves
Habitat:
Kenya and Ethiopia in dry savanna

Warthog
Size:
Length: 2ft 11 to 4 ft 11in.; shoulder height 2 feet. Male weigh 130-330 lbs; Females 99-165 lbs.
Diet:
Meat in the form of grubs, insects, other invertebrates, and will also scavenge dead animals. They also eat grasses, berries, and some crops.
Habitat:
Sub-Saharan Africa, Savannas, in grassland, savanna, and woodlands

Jaguar
Size:
On average length of between 6 and 10 feet, with males rarely reaching 12 - 14 feet. The tail length is almost half of their overall length.
Diet:
Fish, turtles, birds, snakes, frogs, and mammals
Habitat:
Southeastern United States near freshwater lakes, ponds and rivers

Sumatran Tiger
Size:
Grow to Diet: maximum of 9 feet in length weight rages 165-300 pounds
Medium sized mammals, including deer and pigs
Habitat:
The island of Sumatra in Indonesia near lowland forests, mountain forests, and tropical rainforests

Squirrel Monkey
Size:
Adult length: 12.5 in.; tail length: approximately 16 in.
Diet:
Fruit, leaves, insects, frogs and invertebrate
Habitat:
Bolivia, Brazil, Colombia, Ecuador, French Guiana, Guyana, Peru, Suriname, Paraguay, and Venezuela

Southern White Rhinoceros
Size:
Height: 5 to 6 feet at the shoulder; weight – 4,000 to 5,000 lbs.
Diet:
Long and short grasses and herbs
Habitat:
Eastern and southern Africa, from Kenya to South Africa in savannas

Scarlet Ibis
Size:
Adult length: 22 to 24 in.; weight: 1.4 lbs.; wingspan: about 21 in.; coloration: completely scarlet with black wing tips.
Diet:
Insects, crustaceans, mollusks
Habitat:
Tropical South American coastlines in mudflats, shoreline and rainforest

African Spoonbill
Size:
Height: 36; wingspan: 14.4" – 15.9". African spoonbills are all white except for red legs and face and long grey spatulate bill.
Diet:
Long and short grasses and herbs
Habitat:
African Madagascar in Marshy wetlands with some open shallow water like riverbanks, lake shores, marshes, plains, savannas, swamps, and water-meadows.

Whooping Crane
Size:
Adult length: 22 to 24 in.; weight: 1.4 lbs.; wingspan: about 21 in.; coloration: completely scarlet with black wing tips.
Diet:
Insects, crustaceans, mollusks
Habitat:
From central Canada to Mexico, Utah eastward to the Atlantic Coast in the northern tallgrass prairie in Midwest

Emu
Size:
They can grow to be over 6 feet in height, and can weigh over 100 pounds
Diet:
Grass, insects, fruit, and seeds
Habitat:
Australia in forests, grassy plains, and desert areas.

[60]

Mommy said, Wow! You kids did a fantastic job! I am so proud of you for making such a significant effort, and your report is going to be really good."

Dad agreed, "Yes, I am really looking forward to the final reports. I must say, you all made a

zoo trip into a spectacular event. I am looking forward to our next homework trip!"

Dyamond said, "Hey did I tell you all I ran into a classmate, Tanya? She was headed towards the Panda Bears exhibit. She was with her Pa Pa. She looked like she was enjoying the Zoo too."

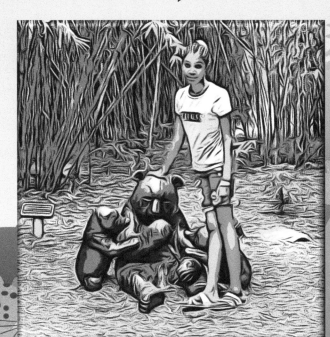

[61]

Vesta said, "I saw my teacher Ms. Greene and her cute assistant Ms. Le'Shae. I wonder if they were trying to follow me to see if I was doing my homework...?"

Dyamond said, "Vesta, no one is following you. How would they even know you were here? You are being silly."

Daddy said, "Alright you guys, be nice, we had a really good day, and we will end it on a really good note."

Dyamond and Vesta both said, "Yes, daddy you are right."

Mommy said, "Well, we have all the pictures we need to go into the reports, so let's get packed up to go home."

The family all got in the mini a to go home.

What about you? Do you know of any animals?
List them in the shapes below...

Tell us about your last Zoo trip in the lines below:

About the Author

Frizella Taylor is a wife, mother, grandmother, ordained minister, author, conference speaker, writing coach and entrepreneur. Frizella's writing career began over 20 years ago. She has composed and written several types of books. Her Christian background has provided her with a wealth of leadership experiences (i.e., children's ministry, youth ministry, women ministry, prayer, and intercessory ministry as well as Pastoral) to glean from and share.

You may find her books at www.TaylorMadePublishingFL.com/frizella-taylor. Frizella's formal education includes a master's degree in Information Technology, Bachelor of Science in Management and Business, and an associate degree in Computer Programming.

Frizella along with her husband, Steve are owners of TaylorMade Publishing LLC of Florida providing services to authors in the areas of coaching, proofreading, editing, formatting, eBook, book publishing, book promotion videos, and author websites. You can learn more about TaylorMade Publishing LLC of Florida on our website: www.TaylorMadePublishingFL.com.

Other children book by Frizella

Lightning Source UK Ltd.
Milton Keynes UK
UKHW051000311022
411374UK00008B/34